DUTCH
Made Nice & Easy!®

Staff of Research & Education Association
Carl Fuchs, Language Program Director

Based on Language Courses developed by the
U.S. Government for Foreign Service Personnel

Research & Education Association
Visit our website at
www.rea.com

Research & Education Association
61 Ethel Road West
Piscataway, New Jersey 08854
E-mail: info@rea.com

DUTCH MADE NICE & EASY®

Printed in the United States of America

Library of Congress Control Number 2006928574

International Standard Book Number 0-87891-399-8

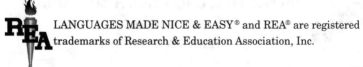

What This Guide Will Do For You

Whether travelling to a foreign country or to your favorite international restaurant, this *Nice & Easy* guide gives you just enough of the language to get around and be understood. Much of the material in this book was developed for government personnel who are often assigned to a foreign country on a moment's notice and need a quick introduction to the language.

In this handy and compact guide, you will find useful words and phrases, popular expressions, common greetings, and the words for numbers, money, and time. Every word or phrase is accompanied with the correct pronunciation and spelling. There is a vocabulary list for finding words quickly.

Generous margins on the pages allow you to make notes and remarks that you may find helpful.

If you expect to travel to the Netherlands, the section on the country's history and relevant up-to-date facts will make your trip more informative and enjoyable. By keeping this guide with you, you'll be well prepared to understand as well as converse in Dutch.

Carl Fuchs
Language Program Director

Contents

NETHERLANDS

FACTS & HISTORY

Official Name: Kingdom of the Netherlands

Geography
Area: 41,526 sq. km. (16,485 sq. mi.).
Cities: *Capital*–Amsterdam (pop. 739,000).
Other cities–The Hague, seat of government (469,000);
Rotterdam, the world's largest port (599,000);
Utrecht (270,000).
Terrain: Coastal lowland.
Climate: Northern maritime.

People
Population: 16.3 million.
Nationality: *Noun*–Dutchmen and Dutchwomen.
Adjective–Dutch.
Ethnic groups: Predominantly Dutch; largest minority communities are Moroccans, Turks, Surinamese.
Religions: Roman Catholic, Protestant, Muslim, other.
Language: Dutch.
Education: *Years compulsory*–10. *Attendance*–nearly 100%. *Literacy*–99%.

Health: *Infant mortality rate*–5.0/1,000.
Life expectancy–78 yrs.
Work force: (7.4 million). *Commercial services*–46.3%;
Non-commercial services–32.4%; *Industry*–19.6%;
Agriculture–1.7%.

Government
Type: Parliamentary democracy under a constitutional monarch.
Constitution: 1814 and 1848.
Branches: *Executive*–monarch (chief of state), prime minister (head of government), cabinet. *Legislative*–bicameral parliament (First and Second Chambers).
Judicial–Supreme Court.
Subdivisions: 12 provinces.

Economy
GDP: $591 billion.
GDP real growth rate: 1.3%.
GDP per capita: $36,236.
Natural resources: Natural gas, petroleum, fertile soil.
Agriculture (2.4% of GDP): *Products*–dairy, poultry, meat, flower bulbs, cut flowers, vegetables and fruits, sugarbeets, potatoes, wheat, barley.
Industry: (25% of GDP): *Types*–agroindustries, steel and aluminum, metal and engineering products, electric machinery and equipment, bulk chemicals, natural gas, petroleum products, transport equipment, microelectronics.

Trade: *Exports*–$313 billion: mineral fuels, chemicals, machinery and transport equipment, processed food and tobacco, agricultural products. *Imports*– $274 billion (c.i.f): mineral fuels and crude petroleum, machinery, transportation equipment, consumer goods, foodstuffs. *Major trading partners*–EU, Germany, Belgium, U.K., U.S.

The Dutch Language

Dutch is the first language of more than 21 million Dutch and Flemish people. A Dutch dialect is spoken by 60,000 people in northwest France. Dutch is also spoken in the Netherlands Antilles and Aruba, which are part of the Kingdom of the Netherlands, and in the former Dutch colony of Suriname, where it is the language of government and education. In the former Dutch East Indies, now the republic of Indonesia, it is still used by lawyers and historians, who need it to consult sources. Afrikaans, which is spoken in South Africa, derives from 17th-century Dutch. Dutch has also influenced other languages, particularly in the areas of shipping, hydraulic engineering and agriculture. In addition, it is taught at almost 250 universities around the world. Dutch is often chosen as a second language in schools in the French-speaking part of Belgium and in northern France and Germany. In 1980, the Netherlands and Flanders founded the Dutch Language Union to foster the study and use of Dutch throughout the world and to set spelling and grammar rules. Frisian, an official minority language, is spoken in the province of Friesland in the northeast of the Netherlands. It is the first language of around 400,000 Frisians and has much in common with English and the Scandinavian languages. Dutch, however, is the language of education throughout the country.

History of the Netherlands

Important Historical Events

57 BC–The Romans invade the Low Countries

70-250 AD–Period of relative peace and prosperity. Roman-occupied area comprises the Netherlands south of the Rhine

768–Beginning of the reign of Charlemagne, founder of the Holy Roman Empire

834-1007–Viking raids

1400-1558–Unification of the Low Countries (the Netherlands and present-day Belgium and Luxembourg) and integration into the Burgundian-Hapsburg Empire

1568–Beginning of the Eighty Years' War: Prince William of Orange leads the Dutch Revolt against Philip II of Spain

1581–The signatory States to the Union of Utrecht abjure Philip II's sovereignty

1588–Republic of the United Provinces established when signatory States to the Union of Utrecht assume sovereign power

1602–The United East India Company (VOC) established

1621–Establishment of the West India Company. From 1620's Dutch colonial expansion, including, New Amsterdam (present-day New York) in North America, the Dutch Antilles, Indonesia, Suriname, the Cape Colony of South Africa, Ceylon and Brazil.

1609-1621–Twelve Years' truce between the Republic and Spain

1648–Peace of Westphalia ends the Dutch Revolt

1652-1674–Anglo-Dutch Wars 1652-54, 1665-67 and 1672-74: the Republic's near monopoly of seaborne trade seen as a threat to England's mercantile interests.

1688-1689–Glorious Revolution in Britain. Prince William III of Orange, Stadholder of the Republic (i.e., head of state), and Mary Stuart ascend the throne of Great Britain as joint monarchs William III and Mary II, creating the constitutional monarchy in Britain.

1700-1780's–Period of economic decline in the Republic and growing mercantile strength in other countries

1780-1784–Fourth Anglo-Dutch War: the Republic suffers a number of naval defeats and loses some colonies. The United East India Company (VOC) is brought to the edge of bankruptcy and disappears in 1798

1806–Louis Napoleon, brother of Napoleon Bonaparte, becomes King of Holland and the Republic is renamed the Kingdom of Holland

1813–Popular uprising against Napoleon. Prince William Frederick of Orange, son of William V, returns from exile and lands at Scheveningen

1830–Belgium gains its independence from the Kingdom

1840–King William I succeeded by his son William II

1848–New constitution drafted bringing greater political power for the Lower House of Parliament and new civil rights, such as freedom of religion and education

1849–King William III ascends the throne

1863–Abolition of slavery

1870–Abolition of the death penalty

1873-1912–The Aceh region of Sumatra in Indonesia rebels against Dutch rule, leading to the Aceh wars

1890–Death of King William III. His widow Emma becomes regent on behalf of their daughter Wilhelmina

1898–Installation of Queen Wilhelmina

1913–Permanent Court of Arbitration established in the Peace Palace in The Hague

1914-1918–First World War. The Netherlands remains neutral

1917–Universal franchise

1940-1945–Second World War. The Netherlands occupied by German forces

Spring 1945–The Netherlands liberated by Canadian and Polish troops

1954–Charter of the Kingdom of the Netherlands establishing the present-day composition of the Kingdom: the Netherlands, the Netherlands Antilles and Aruba

1975–Suriname becomes an independent republic

1986–Aruba secedes from the Netherlands Antilles and acquires separate status within the Kingdom

1990–The Schengen Agreement, to which the Netherlands is a signatory, abolishes internal border controls on the movement of persons between the signatory countries

1991–The Maastricht European Council, under the

Dutch Presidency, concludes the Treaty on European Union

1992–The States-General of the Netherlands ratifies the Maastricht Treaty

1997–Completion of the Delta Project - the last storm-surge barrier is placed in the New Waterway near Europort

The Dutch are primarily of Germanic stock with some Gallo-Celtic mixture. Their small homeland frequently has been threatened with destruction by the North Sea and has often been invaded by the great European powers.

Julius Caesar found the region which is now the Netherlands inhabited by Germanic tribes in the first century B.C. The western portion was inhabited by the Batavians and became part of a Roman province; the eastern portion was inhabited by the Frisians. Between the fourth and eighth centuries A.D., most of both portions were conquered by the Franks. The area later passed into the hands of the House of Burgundy and the Austrian Hapsburgs. Falling under harsh Spanish rule in the 16th century, the Dutch revolted in 1558 under the leadership of Willem of Orange. By virtue of the

Union of Utrecht in 1579, the seven northern Dutch provinces became the Republic of the United Netherlands.

During the 17th century, considered its "golden era," the Netherlands became a great sea and colonial power. Among other achievements, this period saw the emergence of some of painting's "Old Masters," including Rembrandt and Hals, whose works — along with those of later artists such as Mondriaan and Van Gogh — are today on display in museums throughout the Netherlands. The country's importance declined, however, with the gradual loss of Dutch technological superiority and after wars with Spain, France, and England in the 18th century. The Dutch United Provinces supported the Americans in the Revolutionary War. In 1795, French troops ousted Willem V of Orange, the Stadhouder under the Dutch Republic and head of the House of Orange. Following Napoleon's defeat in 1813, the Netherlands and Belgium became the Kingdom of the United Netherlands under King Willem I, son of Willem V of Orange. The Belgians withdrew from the union in 1830 to form their own kingdom. King Willem II was largely responsible for the liberalizing revision of the constitution in 1848.

The Netherlands prospered during the long reign of Willem III (1849-90). At the time of his death, his daughter Wilhelmina was 10 years old. Her mother, Queen Emma, reigned as regent until 1898, when Wilhelmina reached the age of 18 and became the monarch. The Netherlands proclaimed neutrality at the start of both world wars. Although it escaped occupation in World War I, the Netherlands was overrun with German troops in May 1940. Queen Wilhelmina fled to London and established a government-in-exile. Shortly after the Netherlands was liberated in May 1945, the Queen returned. Crown Princess Juliana acceded to the throne in 1948 upon her mother's abdication. In April 1980, Queen Juliana abdicated in favor of her daughter, now Queen Beatrix. Crown Prince Willem Alexander was born in 1967.

Elements of the Netherlands' once far-flung empire were granted either full independence or nearly complete autonomy after World War II. Indonesia formally gained its independence in 1949, and Suriname became independent in 1975. The five islands of the Netherlands Antilles (Curacao, Bonaire, Saba, St. Eustatius, and a part of St. Maarten) and Aruba are integral parts of the Netherlands realm but enjoy a large degree of autonomy.

Delft Town Hall

Royal Palace, Amsterdam

Along canal, Amsterdam

Hints on Pronunciation

All the words and phrases are written in a simplified spelling which you read like English. Each letter or combination of letters is used for the sound it usually stands for in English and it *always* stands for that sound. Thus, *oo* is always pronounced as it is in *too, boot, tooth, roost,* never as anything else. Say these words and then pronounce the vowel sound by itself. That is the sound you must use every time you see *oo* in the *Pronunciation* column. If you should use some other sound—for example, the sound of *oo* in *blood*—you might be misunderstood.

Beurs (Stock exchange), Vlissingen

Koninklijk Paleis, Citizens' Hall, Amsterdam

Syllables that are accented, that is, pronounced louder than others, are written in capital letters. Curved lines (‿) are used to show sounds that are pronounced together without any break; for example, *K‿NO- pun* meaning "buttons."

Special Points

A or AH   stands for the sound in *hot, not, lot*. It often sounds like the *u*-sound in *but*. It is always very short. Example: *DAHT* meaning "that."

Kasteel, Ruurlo

Trompenburgh, Hilversum

AA stands for the sound in *father, calm, pa*. It is
longer than the sound written *a* or *ah*.
Example: *YAA* meaning "yes." When it comes
before *r* some Dutch speakers use a sound
more like that in the English word *wire*.
Example: *WAAR* meaning "where."

U or UH stands for a sound we don't have in English.
To pronounce it you say the *u* in *cut* and at the
same time round your lips as though about to
say the *o* in *go*. Example: *YUF-row* meaning
"miss."

EW   stands for another sound we don't have in English. To make it you say the *ee* in *bee* and at the same time round your lips as though about to say the *oo* in *boo*. Example: *DAHNK ew* meaning "thank you."

AI   stands for a sound made by pronouncing the *a*-sound in *hat* and the *ee*-sound in *feet* together without any pause between the two. Example: *VAIF* meaning "five."

OU and   stand for two different sounds. Example:
OW   *FROUT* meaning "fruit" and *ZOWT* meaning "salt."

<u>H</u> *and* <u>K</u>   both stand for a sound somewhat like the one you make when you clear your throat.
At the beginning of a word or syllable this sound is written <u>h</u>; at the end of a word or syllable it is written <u>k</u>. Example: <u>h</u>oo-dun *DAH<u>K</u>* meaning "Good day."

The Dutch *w*, *v* and *z* may give you a little trouble, for the *w* often sounds like a *v*, the *v* like an *f*, and the *z* like an *s*. Try to imitate the Dutch pronunciation of these sounds, although you will be understood if you use the English pronunciation.

You will notice that many Dutch speakers don't pronounce an *n* when it comes at the end of a word. For instance, you will often hear *hoo-duh MAWR-huh* rather than *hoo-dun MAWR-hun*.

St. Catharijnekerk, Brielle

Muiderslot, Muiden

GREETINGS AND GENERAL PHRASES

English	Pronunciation	Dutch Spelling
Good day	<u>h</u>oo-dun DAH<u>K</u>	Goeden dag
Good morning	<u>h</u>oo-dun MAWR-<u>h</u>un	Goeden morgen
Good evening	<u>h</u>oo-dun AA-vawnt	Goeden avond

In the expression *<u>h</u>oo-dun DAH<u>K</u>* you hear a sound you must practice. It is written in your *Language Guide* as *h* underlined when it begins a word or syl-

English	Pronunciation	Dutch Spelling

lable and as _k_ underlined when it comes at the end. Listen and repeat: _hoo-dun DAHK_, _hoo-dun DAHK_. It is like clearing your throat. Try just the sound again: _h_, _h_.

Sir *or* **Mr.**	_muh-NAYR_	Mijnheer
Madam *or* **Mrs.**	_muv-ROW_	Mevrouw
Miss	_yuf-ROW_	Juffrouw

When this word is used with a person's name, the first syllable is accented.

Miss Smit	_YUF-row SMIT_	Juffrouw Smit
How are you?	_hoo HAAT ut met EW?_	Hoe gaat het met U?
Fine	_HOOT_	Goed
Thank you	_DAHNK ew_	Dank U

You have just heard two more sounds you must practice. The first which you heard in _YUF-row_ is written in your *Guide* as _u_ [and._uh_]; the second you heard in _DAHNK ew_ and it is written _ew_. The _u_ is like our _u_ in _cut_ but you round your lips at the same time; the _ew_ is like the _ee_-sound of _feet_ but you round your lips here too. Listen and repeat: _yuf-ROW_, _yuf-ROW; DAHNK ew_, _DAHNK ew_. Try just the sounds again: _u_, _u; ew_, _ew_.

11

English	Pronunciation	Dutch Spelling
You're welcome	*tawt ew DEENST*	Tot Uw dienst
Please	*ahss-tew-BLEEFT*	Alstublieft

Always use *ahss-tew-BLEEFT* when you ask a favor. If you do, the Dutch people will be eager to help you.

Excuse me	*par-DAWN*	Pardon
Yes	*YAA*	Ja
No	*NAY*	Neen
Do you under-stand?	*vur-STAAT ew ut?*	Verstaat U het?
I understand	*ik vur-STAA ut*	Ik versta het
I don't under-stand	*ik vur-STAA ut NEET*	Ik versta het niet
Speak slowly	*SPRAYKT ew LAHNK-zaam*	Spreekt U langzaam

In the last word you heard two sounds you must learn to distinguish. The first is written *a* or *ah* in your *Guide* and sounds at times to us like the *u* of *cut*. Be sure you make it short. The other is written with two *a*'s and is much longer. Listen and repeat: *LAHNK-zaam, LAHNK-zaam.* Try just the sounds again: *ah, ah; aa, aa.*

12

English	Pronunciation	Dutch Spelling

LOCATION

When you need directions to get somewhere use the phrase "Where is" and then add the words you need.

English	Pronunciation	Dutch Spelling
Where is a restaurant	*WAAR ISS un RESS-to-rahnt*	Waar is een restaurant
Where is a restaurant?	*WAAR ISS un RESS-to-rahnt?*	Waar is een restaurant?
Where is a hotel?	*WAAR ISS un ho-TEL?*	Waar is een hotel?
Where is the railroad station?	*WAAR ISS ut staash-YAWN?*	Waar is het station?
Where is the toilet?	*WAAR ISS duh WAY SAY?*	Waar is de W. C.?

Huize Nienoord, Leek

English	*Pronunciation*	*Dutch Spelling*

DIRECTIONS

The answer to your question "Where is such and such?" may be "To the right" or "To the left" or "Straight ahead," so you need to know these phrases.

To the right	*naar REKTS*	Naar rechts
To the left	*naar LINKS*	Naar links
Straight ahead	*REKT-out*	Rechtuit

It is sometimes useful to say "Point out the way."

Point out the way to me	*WILT ew muh duh WEK WAI-zun?*	Wilt U mij den weg wijzen?

If you are driving and ask the distance to another town it will be given to you in kilometers, not miles.

kilometer	*kee-lo-MAY-tur*	kilometer

One kilometer equals ⅝ of a mile.

"The Night Watch," Rembrandt

English	*Pronunciation*	*Dutch Spelling*

NUMBERS

You need to know the numbers.

One	*AYN*	een
Two	*TWAY*	twee
Three	*DREE*	drie
Four	*VEER*	vier
Five	*VAIF*	vijf

Notice the sound written *ai* in the last word. Listen and repeat: *VAIF, VAIF.* To make this sound you put an *a*-sound [as in *hat*] and an *ee*-sound together without any pause between the two. Try just the sound again: *ai, ai.*

15

English	Pronunciation	Dutch Spelling
Six	*ZESS*	zes
Seven	*ZAY-vun*	zeven
Eight	*AHKT*	acht
Nine	*NAY-hun*	negen
Ten	*TEEN*	tien
Eleven	*EL-uf*	elf
Twelve	*TWAA-luf*	twaalf
Thirteen	*DEHR-teen*	dertien
Fourteen	*VAYR-teen*	veertien
Fifteen	*VAIF-teen*	vijftien
Sixteen	*ZESS-teen*	zestien
Seventeen	*ZAY-vun-teen*	zeventien
Eighteen	*AHK-teen*	achttien
Nineteen	*NAY-hun-teen*	negentien
Twenty	*TWIN-tuk*	twintig

For "twenty-one," "twenty-two," etc., you say "one and twenty," "two and twenty," etc.

Twenty-one	*AYN-en-twin-tuk*	een-en-twintig
Twenty-two	*TWAY-en-twin-tuk*	twee-en-twintig
Thirty	*DEHR-tuk*	dertig

English	Pronunciation	Dutch Spelling
Forty	*VAYR-tuk*	veertig
Fifty	*VAIF-tuk*	vijftig
Sixty	*ZESS-tuk*	zestig
Seventy	*ZAY-vun-tuk*	zeventig
Eighty	*TAHK-tuk*	tachtig
Ninety	*NAY-hun-tuk*	negentig
Hundred	*HAWN-durt*	honderd
Thousand	*DOU-zunt*	duizend

Castle, Zeist

Dordrecht

English	Pronunciation	Dutch Spelling

WHAT'S THIS?

When you want to know the name of something you can say "What's this [or that]?" and point to the thing you mean.

What is that [this]	*WAHT ISS DAHT [DIT]*	Wat is dat [dit]
What's that?	*waht IZ daht?*	Wat is dat?
[What's this?]	*[waht IZ dit?]*	[Wat is dit?]

ASKING FOR THINGS

When you want something to eat you can say:

I would like to eat	*ik WIL ḫraaḫ A Y-tun*	Ik wil graag eten

English	Pronunciation	Dutch Spelling
I would like to eat	*ik WIL hraak A Y-tun*	Ik wil graag eten

To ask for something use the name of the thing wanted and then add the word for "please"— *ahss-tew-BLEEFT*.

cigarettes	*see-haa-RET-un*	cigaretten
Cigarettes, please	*see-haa-RET-un, ahss-tew-BLEEFT*	Cigaretten, ·alstublieft
matches	*LEW-see-vayrss*	lucifers
Matches, please	*LEW-see-vayrss, ahss-tew-BLEEFT*	Lucifers, alstublieft

Here are the words for some of the things you may require.

bread	*BROHT*	brood
butter	*BO-tur*	boter
soup	*SOOP*	soep
fish	*VISS*	vis
meat	*VLAYSS*	vlees
beefsteak	*BEEF-stuk*	biefstuk
pork	*VAR-kunz-vlayss*	varkensvlees
veal	*KAHL-ufs-vlayss*	kalfsvlees

English	Pronunciation	Dutch Spelling
eggs	*AI-run*	eieren
vegetables	*HROON-tun*	groenten
potatoes	*AAR-dahp-ul-un*	aardappelen
beans	*BO-nun*	bonen
cabbage	*KOHL*	kool
salt	*ZOWT*	zout
sugar	*SOU-kur*	suiker
fruit	*FROUT*	fruit

Notice the difference between the sounds written in your *Guide* as *ou* and *ow*. Listen and repeat in the words for *fruit* and *salt: FROUT, FROUT; ZOWT, ZOWT.*

apples	*AHP-ul-un*	appelen
milk	*MEL-uk*	melk
water	*WAA-tur*	water

The Dutch *w*-sound is a little like our *v* and the Dutch *v* sometimes sounds a little like our *f*, but if you listen to the words for "water," "fish" and "fruit," you will hear the difference between the *w*, *v* and *f*: water—*WAA-tur, WAA-tur;* fish—*VISS, VISS;* fruit—*FROUT, FROUT.*

English	Pronunciation	Dutch Spelling
tea	*TAY*	thee
a cup of coffee	*un kawp KAWF-ee*	een kop koffie
a glass of beer	*un ḫlahss BEER*	een glas bier

MONEY

To find out how much things cost you say:

How much	*hoo-VAYL*	Hoeveel
costs	*KAWST*	kost
this	*DIT*	dit
How much does this cost?	*HOO-vayl KAWST dit?*	Hoeveel kost dit?

TIME

When you want to know what time it is you say really "How late is it?"

Rijksmuseum, Amsterdam

21

English	Pronunciation	Dutch Spelling
What time is it?	*hoo LAAT iz ut?*	Hoe laat is het?
One o'clock	*AYN EWR*	een uur

For "ten past two" and "quarter past three" you say "ten over two" and "quarter over three."

Ten past two	*TEEN o-vur TWAY*	tien over twee
Quarter past three	*KWART o-vur DREE*	kwart over drie

"Half past four" is "half five."

Half past four	*HAHL-uf VAIF*	half vijf

For "quarter of five" and "five minutes of six" you say "quarter before five" and "five before six."

Quarter of five	*KWART vohr VAIF*	kwart voor vijf
Five of six	*VAIF vohr ZESS*	vijf voor zes

When you want to know when a movie starts or when a train leaves you say:

At what time	*hoo LAAT*	Hoe laat
begins	*buh-HINT*	begint
the movie	*duh bee-o-SKOHP*	de bioscoop

English	Pronunciation	Dutch Spelling
When does the movie start?	*hoo LAAT buh-HINT duh bee-o-SKOHP?*	Hoe laat begint de bioscoop?
leaves	*vur-TREKT*	vertrekt
the train	*duh TRAIN*	de trein
When does the train leave?	*hoo LAAT vur-TREKT duh TRAIN?*	Hoe laat vertrekt de trein?
Yesterday	*HISS-tur-un*	gisteren
Today	*vahn-DAAK*	vandaag
Tomorrow	*MAWR-hun*	morgen

The days of the week are:

Sunday	*ZAWN-dahk*	Zondag
Monday	*MAAN-dahk*	Maandag
Tuesday	*DINZ-dahk*	Dinsdag
Wednesday	*WOONZ-dahk*	Woensdag
Thursday	*DAWN-dur-dahk*	Donderdag
Friday	*VRAI-dahk*	Vrijdag
Saturday	*ZAA-tur-dahk*	Zaterdag

23

Amersfoort, Koppelport

English	Pronunciation	Dutch Spelling

OTHER USEFUL PHRASES

The following phrases will be useful:

English	Pronunciation	Dutch Spelling
What is your name?	*hoo HAYT ew?*	Hoe heet U?
My name is___	*main NAAM iss___*	Mijn naam is___
How do you say *table* (or anything else) in Dutch?	*hoo ZEKT ew* table *in ut HAW-lahnts?*	Hoe zegt U *table* in het Hollands?
I am an American	*ik BEN un ah-may-ree-KAAN*	Ik ben een Amerikaan

English	Pronunciation	Dutch Spelling
I am your friend	*ik BEN ew VREENT*	Ik ben Uw vriend
Please help me	*HEL-upt ew muh, ahss-tew-BLEEFT*	Helpt U mij, alstublieft
Take me there	*WILT ew muh DAAR naar TOO BRENG-un?*	Wilt U mij daar naar toe brengen?
Good-by	*tawt ZEENSS*	Tot ziens

A common expression used like our "So long" is:

DAHK̲ Dag

Spaarne with weigh-house, Haarlem

25

ADDITIONAL
EXPRESSIONS

English	*Pronunciation*	*Dutch Spelling*
Come in!	*KAWM BIN-un!*	Kom binnen!
Have a seat!	*H̲AA ZIT-un!*	Ga zitten!
Glad to know you	*AAN-h̲uh-naam*	Aangenaam
Will you repeat?	*WILT ew ut hur-H̲AA-lun?*	Wilt U het herhalen?
I don't know	*ik WAYT ut neet*	Ik weet het niet
I think so	*ik h̲uh-LOHF vahn WEL*	Ik geloof van wel
I don't think so	*ik h̲uh-LOHF vahn NEET*	Ik geloof van niet
Maybe	*miss-H̲EEN*	Misschien
Stop!	*STAWP!*	Stop!
Come here!	*KAWMT ew HEER!*	Komt U hier!
Quickly!	*VLUK̲!*	Vlug!
Come quickly!	*KAWMT ew VLUK̲!*	Komt U vlug!
Go quickly!	*H̲AAT ew VLUK̲!*	Gaat U vlug!
I am hungry	*IK hep HAWNG-ur*	Ik heb honger
I am thirsty	*IK hep DAWRST*	Ik heb dorst

26

English	Pronunciation	Dutch Spelling
I am tired	*IK ben MOO*	Ik ben moe
I am lost	*IK ben vur-DWAALT*	Ik ben verdwaald
Help!	*HEL-up!*	Help!
Bring help!	*BRENKT ew HUL-up!*	Brengt U hulp!
I shall pay you	*ik ZAHL ew buh-TAA-lun*	Ik zal U betalen
Which way is north?	*WAAR ISS ut NOHR-dun?*	Waar is het noorden?
Which is the road to___?	*WEL-kuh WEK ḫaat naar___?*	Welke weg gaat naar___?
Will you draw a map?	*WILT ew un KAART TAYK-nun?*	Wilt U een kaart tekenen?
Will you take me to a doctor?	*WILT ew muh naar un DAWK-tur BRENG-un?*	Wilt U mij naar een dokter brengen?

English	Pronunciation	Dutch Spelling
Will you take me to the hospital?	*WILT ew muh naar ut ZEE-kun-houss BRENG-un?*	Wilt U mij naar het ziekenhuis brengen?
Where is the town?	*WAAR ISS ut DAWRP?*	Waar is het dorp?
Where is the city?	*WAAR ISS duh STAHT?*	Waar is de stad?
How far is it?	*hoo VEHR iss ut?*	Hoe ver is het?
Is it far?	*ISS ut VEHR?*	Is het ver?
Is it near?	*ISS ut DIKT-bai?*	Is het dichtbij?
Danger!	*huh-VAAR!*	Gevaar!
Watch out!	*LET awp!*	Let op!
Wait a minute!	*WAHKT ay-vun!*	Wacht even!
Good luck!	*ut BEST-uh!*	Het beste!

FILL-IN SENTENCES

In this section you will find a number of sentences, each containing a blank space which can be filled in with any one of the words in the list that follows. For example, to say "May I have some drinking water?" look for the phrase "May I have___?" in the English column and find the Dutch expression given beside it: *MAHK ik___HEB-un?* Then look for "drinking water" in the list that follows; the Dutch is *DRINK-waa-tur.* Put this phrase in the blank space and you get *MAHK ik DRINK-waa-tur HEB-un?*

Notice that the order of words in Dutch is sometimes different from the order in English. For example, instead of saying "May I have drinking water?" what you say in Dutch is "May I drinking water have?"

English	Pronunciation	Dutch Spelling
May I have___?	*MAHK ik___ HEB-un?*	Mag ik___hebben?*
May we have___?	*MO-hun wuh___ HEB-un?*	Mogen wij___ hebben?

*The Dutch don't say "I want cigarettes" or "Give me cigarettes," but "Cigarettes, please," "May I have some cigarettes?" or "Will you give me some cigarettes?" Always add the word for "please"—*ahss-tew-BLEEFT.*

Kasteel, Gemert (Helmond)

"The Starry Night," Vincent Van Gogh

English	Pronunciation	Dutch Spelling
Will you bring me___?	*WILT ew muh___ BRENG-un?*	Wilt U mij___ brengen?
Will you give me___?	*WILT ew muh___ HAY-vun?*	Wilt U mij___ geven?
Where can I get___?	*WAAR kahn ik___ KRAI-hun?*	Waar kan ik___ krijgen?
I have___	*ik HEP___*	Ik heb___
We have___	*wuh HEB-un___*	Wij hebben___
Have you___?	*HAYFT ew___?*	Heeft U___?

Example

May I have___?	*MAHK ik___ HEB-un?*	Mag ik___hebben?
drinking water	*DRINK-waa-tur*	drinkwater
May I have some drink- ing water?	*MAHK ik DRINK- waa-tur HEB-un?*	Mag ik drinkwater hebben?
bacon	*SPEK*	spek
boiled water	*huh-KOHKT WAA-tur*	gekookt water
carrots	*WAWR-tulss*	wortels

English	Pronunciation	Dutch Spelling
cheese	*KAASS*	kaas
chicken	*KIP*	kip
chocolate	*sho-ko-LAA-duh*	chocolade
drinking water	*DRINK-waa-tur*	drinkwater
grapes	*DROU-vun*	druiven
ham	*HAHM*	ham
onions	*OU-yun*	uien
pears	*PAY-run*	peren
peas	*EHR-tun*	erwten
strawberries	*AART-bay-un*	aardbeien

(For other foods see pp. 19-20.)

a cup	*un KAWP*	een kop
a fork	*un VAWRK*	een vork
a glass	*un HLAHSS*	een glas
a knife	*un MESS*	een mes
a plate	*un BAWRT*	een bord
a spoon	*un LAY-pul*	een lepel
a bed	*un BET*	een bed

English	Pronunciation	Dutch Spelling
blankets	*DAY-kunss*	dekens
a mattress	*un ma-TRAHSS*	een matras
a mosquito net	*un KLAHM-boo*	een klamboe
a pillow	*un KUSS-un*	een kussen
a room	*un KAA-mur*	een kamer
sheets	*LAA-kunss*	lakens
a towel	*un HAHN-dook*	een handdoek
cigars	*see-HAA-run*	cigaren
a pipe	*un PAIP*	een pijp
tobacco	*TA-bahk*	tabak
a bicycle	*un FEETS*	een fiets
gasoline	*ben-ZEE-nuh*	benzine
ink	*INKT*	inkt
paper	*pa-PEER*	papier
a pen	*un PEN*	een pen
a pencil	*un PAWT-loht*	een potlood
a comb	*un KAHM*	een kam

English	Pronunciation	Dutch Spelling
hot water	*WAHRM WAA-tur*	warm water
a razor	*un SKAYR-mess*	een scheermes
razor blades	*SKAYR-mesh-yuss*	scheermesjes
a shaving brush	*un SKAYR-kwahst*	een scheerkwast
shaving soap	*SKAYR-zayp*	scheerzeep
soap	*ZAYP*	zeep
a toothbrush	*un TAHN-dun-bawr-stul*	een tandenborstel
tooth paste	*TAHNT-pa-staa*	tandpasta
a handkerchief	*un ZAHK-dook*	een zakdoek
a raincoat	*un RAY-hun-yahss*	een regenjas
a shirt	*un HEMT*	een hemd
shoe laces	*SKOON-vay-turss*	schoenveters
shoe polish	*SKOON-smayr*	schoensmeer
shoes	*SKOO-nun*	schoenen
underwear	*AWN-dur-hoot*	ondergoed
buttons	*K̮NO-pun*	knopen

English	Pronunciation	Dutch Spelling
a needle	*un NAALT*	een naald
safety pins	*VAY-luk-haits-spel-dun*	veiligheidsspelden
thread	*DRAAT*	draad
adhesive tape	*PLAI-stur*	pleister
antiseptic	*un ahn-tee-SEP-tiss mid-dul*	een antiseptisch middel
aspirin	*ah-spee-REEN*	aspirine
a bandage	*un vur-BAHNT*	een verband
cotton	*WAHT-un*	watten
a disinfectant	*un dess-in-FEKT-see-mid-ul*	een desinfectie-middel
iodine	*YO-dee-um*	jodium
a laxative	*un lahk-SAYR-mid-ul*	een laxeermiddel
I would like to___	*ik WIL HRAAK___*	Ik wil graag___

Example

I would like to___	*ik WIL HRAAK___*	Ik wil graag___
eat	*AY-tun*	eten

34

English	Pronunciation	Dutch Spelling
I would like to eat	*ik WIL HRAAK A Y-tur*	Ik wil graag eten
pay	*buh-TAA-lun*	betalen
drink	*DRINK-un*	drinken
rest	RUST-*un*	rusten
sleep	*SLAA-pun*	slapen
have my hair cut	*mun HAAR laa-tun K_NIP-un*	mijn haar laten knippen

Bergen op Zoom, Stadhuis

English	Pronunciation	Dutch Spelling
	Example	
I would like to___	*ik WIL___ HRAAK___*	Ik wil___graag
be shaved	*muh___laa-tun SKAY-run*	mij___laten scheren
I would like to be shaved	*ik WIL muh HRAAK laa-tun SKAY-run*	Ik wil mij graag laten scheren
buy it	*ut___ KO-pun*	het___kopen
take a bath	*muh___BAA-dun*	mij___baden
wash up	*muh___WAHSS-un*	mij___wassen
Where is there___?	*WAAR ISS ur___?*	Waar is er___?

	Example	
Where is there___?	*WAAR ISS ur___?*	Waar is er___?
a barber	*un bar-BEER*	een barbier
Where is there a barber?	*WAAR ISS ur un bar-BEER?*	Waar is er een barbier?

36

English	Pronunciation	Dutch Spelling
a dentist	*un TAHNT-arts*	een tandarts
a doctor	*un DAWK-tur*	een dokter
a mechanic	*un may-ka-neesh-YEN*	een mecanicien
a policeman	*un po-LEET-see-ah-ḥent*	een politieagent
a porter	*un KROU-yur*	een kruier
a shoemaker	*un SK̲OON-maa-kur*	een schoenmaker
a tailor	*un KLAYR-maa-kur*	een kleermaker
a workman	*un AR-bai-dur*	een arbeider
a church	*un KEHRK*	een kerk
a clothing store	*un KLAYR-un-wink-ul*	een klerenwinkel
a farm	*un boor-duh-RAI*	een boerderij
a garage	*un ḥa-RAA-juh*	een garage
a grocery	*un krou-duh-NEERSS-wink-ul*	een kruideniers-winkel
a house	*un HOUSS*	een huis
a laundry	*un wahss-uh-RAI*	een wasserij

37

English	Pronunciation	Dutch Spelling
a pharmacy	*un ah-po-TAYK*	een apotheek
a well	*un PUT*	een put
Where is___?	*WAAR ISS___?*	Waar is___?
How far is___?	*hoo VEHR iss___?*	Hoe ver is___?

Example

English	Pronunciation	Dutch Spelling
How far is___? the bridge	*hoo VEHR iss___? duh BRUK*	Hoe ver is___? de brug
How far is the bridge?	*hoo VEHR iss duh BRUK?*	Hoe ver is de brug?
the boat	*duh BOHT*	de boot
the bus	*duh BUSS*	de bus
the camp	*ut KAHMP*	het kamp
the canal	*ut ka-NAAL*	het kanaal
the city	*duh STAHT*	de stad
the filling station	*ut ben-ZEE-nuh-staash-yawn*	het benzinestation
the harbor	*duh HAA-vun*	de haven

38

English	Pronunciation	Dutch Spelling
the highway	*duh HOHFT-wek*	de hoofdweg
the hospital	*ut ZEE-kun-houss*	het ziekenhuis
the main street	*duh HOHFT-straat*	de hoofdstraat
the marketplace	*ut MARKT-plain*	het marktplein
the nearest town	*ut DIKST-bai-zain-duh DAWRP*	het dichstbijzijnde dorp
the police station	*ut po-LEET-see-bew-ro*	het politiebureau
the post office	*ut PAWST-kahn-tohr*	het postkantoor
the railroad	*duh SPOHR-wek*	de spoorweg
the road	*duh WEK*	de weg
the river	*duh ree-VEER*	de rivier
the street car	*duh TREM*	de tram
the telephone	*duh tul-uh-FOHN*	de telefoon
the telegraph office	*ut tul-uh-HRAAF-kahn-tohr*	het telegraafkantoor
the village	*ut DAWRP*	het dorp

English	Pronunciation	Dutch Spelling
I am____	*ik BEN____*	Ik ben____
He is____	*hai ISS____*	Hij is____
We are____	*wuh ZAIN____*	Wij zijn____
They are____	*zuh ZAIN____*	zij zijn____
Are you____?	*BENT ew____?*	Bent U____?

Example

I am____ sick	*ik BEN____* *ZEEK*	Ik ben____ ziek
I am sick	*IK ben ZEEK*	Ik ben ziek
wounded	*ḫuh-WAWNT*	gewond
lost	*vur-DWAALT*	verdwaald
tired	*MOO*	moe
Is it____?	*ISS ut____?*	Is het____?
It is____	*TISS____*	Het is____
It is not____	*tiss NEET____*	Het is niet____
That is____	*DAHT iss____*	Dat is____
This is____	*DIT iss____*	Dit is____

English	Pronunciation	Dutch Spelling
This is too___	*DIT iss tuh___*	Dit is te___
This is not___	*DIT iss NEET___*	Dit is niet___
This is very___	*DIT iss HAYL___*	Dit is heel___

Example

It is not___	*tiss NEET___*	Het is niet___
good	*HOOT*	goed
It is not good	*tiss NEET hoot*	Het is niet goed
bad	*SLEKT*	slecht
cheap	*HOOT-kohp*	goedkoop
expensive	*DEWR*	duur
large	*HROHT*	groot
small	*KLAIN*	klein
clean	*SKOHN*	schoon
dirty	*VOUL*	vuil
cold	*KOWT*	koud
warm	*WAHRM*	warm

Amsterdamse Poort, Haarlem

"Woman with Jug," Jan Vermeer

Zuidhavenpoort, Zierikzee

English	Pronunciation	Dutch Spelling
few	*WAI-nuk̲*	weinig
much (many)	*VAYL*	veel
far	*VEHR*	ver
near	*DIK̲T-bai*	dichtbij
here	*HEER*	hier
there	*DAAR*	daar

42

IMPORTANT SIGNS

Dutch	English
Halt!	Stop!
Langzaam rijden	Slow
Omrijden	Detour
Voorzichtig	Caution
Een richting	One Way
Geen doorrit	No Thoroughfare
Overweg	Grade Crossing
Geen doorgang	Dead End
Rechts houden	Keep to the Right
Gevaarlijke bocht	Dangerous Curve
Spoorweg	Railroad
Brug	Bridge
Kruisweg	Crossroad
Levensgevaarlijk (Hoog-spanning)	High Tension Lines
Geen toegang	Keep Out
Verboden toegang	No Admittance
Parkeren verboden	No Parking
Verboden te roken	No Smoking

Dutch	English
W.C. *or* Retirade	*Lavatory*
Heren	*Men*
Dames	*Women*
Open	*Open*
Gesloten	*Closed*
Ingang	*Entrance*
Uitgang	*Exit*

Kasteel, Mheer (Maastricht)

Stadhuis, Delft

ALPHABETICAL WORD LIST

English	Pronunciation	Dutch Spelling

A

English	Pronunciation	Dutch Spelling
adhesive tape	*PLAI-stur*	pleister
am		
I am___	*ik BEN___*	Ik ben___
American		
I am an American	*ik BEN un ah-may-ree-KAAN*	Ik ben een Amerikaan
antiseptic	*ahn-tee-SEP-tiss mid-ul*	antiseptisch middel
apples	*AHP-ul-un*	appelen
are		
Are you___?	*BENT ew___?*	Bent U___?
They are___	*zuh ZAIN___*	Zij zijn___
We are___	*wuh ZAIN___*	Wij zijn___
aspirin	*ah-spee-REEN*	aspirine
at what time	*hoo LAAT*	hoe laat

English	Pronunciation	Dutch Spelling

B

English	Pronunciation	Dutch Spelling
bacon	*SPEK*	spek
bad	*SLEKT*	slecht
bandage	*vur-BAHNT*	verband
barber	*bar-BEER*	barbier
bath		
I would like to take a bath	*ik WIL muh HRAAK BAA-dun*	Ik wil mij graag baden
beans	*BO-nun*	bonen
bed	*BET*	bed
beefsteak	*BEEF-stuk*	biefstuk
beer	*BEER*	bier
a glass of beer	*un hlahss BEER*	een glas bier
begin		
When does the movie begin?	*hoo LAAT buh-HINT duh bee-o-SKOHP?*	Hoe laat begint de bioscoop?
bicycle	*FEETS*	fiets
blades		
razor blades	*SKAYR-mesh-yuss*	scheermesjes

English	Pronunciation	Dutch Spelling
blankets	*DAY-kunss*	dekens
boat	*BOHT*	boot
boiled water	*ḫuh-KOHKT WAA-tur*	gekookt water
bread	*BROHT*	brood
bridge	*BRUK̲*	brug
bring		
Bring help!	*BRENKT ew HUL-up!*	Brengt U hulp!
Will you bring me___?	*WILT ew muh___ BRENG-un?*	Wilt U mij___ brengen?
brush	*BAWR-stul*	borstel
shaving brush	*SK̲AYR-kwahst*	scheerkwast
toothbrush	*TAHN-dun-bawr-stul*	tandenborstel
bus	*BUSS*	bus
butter	*BO-tur*	boter
buttons	*K̲NO-pun*	knopen
buy		
I would like to buy it	*ik WIL ut ḪRAAK̲ KO-pun*	Ik wil het graag kopen

English	Pronunciation	Dutch Spelling
	C	
cabbage	*KOHL*	kool
camp	*KAHMP*	kamp
Where is the camp?	*WAAR iss ut KAHMP?*	Waar is het kamp?
can		
Where can I get___?	*WAAR kahn ik___ KRAI-ḫun?*	Waar kan ik___ krijgen?
canal	*ka-NAAL*	kanaal
carrots	*WAWR-tulss*	wortels
cent	*SENT*	cent
cheap	*ḪOOT-kohp*	goedkoop
cheese	*KAASS*	kaas
chicken	*KIP*	kip
chocolate	*sho-ko-LAA-duh*	chocolade
church	*KEHRK*	kerk
cigarettes	*see-ḫaa-RET-un*	cigaretten
cigars	*see-ḪAA-run*	cigaren
city	*STAHT*	stad
clean	*SḴOHN*	schoon
clothing store	*KLAYR-un-wink-ul*	klerenwinkel

English	Pronunciation	Dutch Spelling
coffee	*KAWF-ee*	koffie
a cup of coffee	*un kawp KAWF-ee*	een kop koffie
cold	*KOWT*	koud
comb	*KAHM*	kam
come		
Come here!	*KAWMT ew HEER!*	Komt U hier!
Come in!	*KAWM BIN-un!*	Kom binnen!
Come quickly!	*KAWMT ew VLUK!*	Komt U vlug!
cost		
How much does this cost?	*HOO-vayl KAWST dit?*	Hoeveel kost dit?
cotton	*WAHT-un*	watten
cup	*KAWP*	kop
a cup of coffee	*un kawp KAWF-ee*	een kop koffie

D

Danger!	*huh-VAAR!*	Gevaar!

English	Pronunciation	Dutch Spelling
day	*DAHK*	dag
Good day	*hoo-dun DAHK*	Goeden dag
dentist	*TAHNT-arts*	tandarts
dirty	*VOUL*	vuil
disinfectant	*dess-in-FEKT-see-mid-ul*	desinfectiemiddel
doctor	*DAWK-tur*	dokter
Will you take me to a doctor?	*WILT ew muh naar un DAWK-tur BRENG-un?*	Wilt U mij naar een dokter brengen?
draw		
Will you draw a map?	*WILT ew un KAART TAYK-nun?*	Wilt U een kaart tekenen?
drink		
I would like to drink	*ik WIL HRAAK DRINK-un*	Ik wil graag drinken
drinking water	*DRINK-waa-tur*	drinkwater
Dutch	*HAW-lahnts*	Hollands
in Dutch	*in ut HAW-lahnts*	in het Hollands

E

eat		
I would like to eat	*ik WIL HRAAK AY-tun*	Ik wil graag eten

51

English	Pronunciation	Dutch Spelling
eggs	*AI-run*	eieren
eight	*AHK̲T*	acht
eighteen	*AHK̲-teen*	achttien
eighty	*TAHK̲-tuk̲*	tachtig
eleven	*EL-uf*	elf
evening	*AA-vawnt*	avond
Good evening	*ḥoo-dun AA-vawnt*	Goeden avond
Excuse me	*par-DAWN*	Pardon
expensive	*DEWR*	duur

F

far	*VEHR*	ver
How far is___?	*hoo VEHR iss___?*	Hoe ver is___?
Is it far?	*ISS ut VEHR?*	Is het ver?
farm	*boor-duh-RAI*	boerderij
few	*WAI-nuk̲*	weinig
fifteen	*VAIF-teen*	vijftien
fifty	*VAIF-tuk̲*	vijftig
filling station	*ben-ZEE-nuh-staash-yawn*	benzinestation

English	Pronunciation	Dutch Spelling
fine	_HOOT_	goed
fish	_VISS_	vis
five	_VAIF_	vijf
fork	_VAWRK_	vork
forty	_VAYR-tuk_	veertig
four	_VEER_	vier
fourteen	_VAYR-teen_	veertien
Friday	_VRAI-dahk_	Vrijdag
friend	_VREENT_	vriend
I am your friend	_ik BEN ew VREENT_	Ik ben Uw vriend
fruit	_FROUT_	fruit

G

garage	_ha-RAA-juh_	garage
gasoline	_ben-ZEE-nuh_	benzine
get		
Where can I get___?	_WAAR kahn ik___ KRAI-hun?_	Waar kan ik___ krijgen?

53

English	Pronunciation	Dutch Spelling
give		
Will you give me____?	*WILT ew muh___ HAY-vun?*	Wilt U mij____geven?
Glad to know you	*AAN-huh-naam*	Aangenaam
glass	*HLAHSS*	glas
a glass of beer	*un hlahss BEER*	een glas bier
go		
Go quickly!	*HAAT ew VLUK!*	Gaat U vlug!
good	*HOOT*	goed
Good day	*hoo-dun DAHK*	Goeden dag
Good evening	*hoo-dun AA-vawnt*	Goeden avond
Good luck!	*ut BEST-uh!*	Het beste!
Good morning	*hoo-dun MAWR-hun*	Goeden morgen
Good-by	*tawt ZEENSS*	Tot ziens
grapes	*DROU-vun*	druiven
grocery	*krou-duh-NEERSS-wink-ul*	kruidenierswinkel

English	Pronunciation	Dutch Spelling
	H	
hair	*HAAR*	haar
I would like to have my hair cut	*ik WIL H̱RAAḴ mun HAAR laa-tun Ḵ_NIP-un*	Ik wil graag mijn haar laten knippen
half	*HAHL-uf*	half
half past four	*HAHL-uf VAIF*	half vijf
ham	*HAHM*	ham
handkerchief	*ZAHK-dook*	zakdoek
harbor	*HAA-vun*	haven
have		
Do you have___?	*HAYFT ew___?*	Heeft U___?
Have a seat!	*H̱AA ZIT-un!*	Ga zitten!
I have___	*ik HEP___*	Ik heb___
May I have___?	*MAHḴ ik___ HEB̄-un?*	Mag ik___hebben?
May we have___?	*MO-ḥun wuh___ HEB̄-un?*	Mogen wij___ hebben?
We have___	*wuh HEB-un___*	Wij hebben___

English	Pronunciation	Dutch Spelling
he	*HAI*	hij
He is___	*hai ISS___*	Hij is___
Help!	*HEL-up!*	Help!
Bring help!	*BRENKT ew HUL-up!*	Brengt U hulp!
Please help me!	*HEL-upt ew muh, ahss-tew-BLEEFT!*	Helpt U mij, alstublieft!
here	*HEER*	hier
Come here!	*KAWMT ew HEER!*	Komt U hier!
highway	*HOHFT-wek̲*	hoofdweg
hospital	*ZEE-kun-houss*	ziekenhuis
Will you take me to the hospital?	*WILT ew muh naar ut ZEE-kun-houss BRENG-un?*	Wilt U mij naar het ziekenhuis brengen?
hot water	*WAHRM WAA-tur*	warm water
hotel	*ho-TEL*	hotel
Where is a hotel?	*WAAR ISS un ho-TEL?*	Waar is een hotel?
house	*HOUSS*	huis
how	*HOO*	hoe
How are you?	*hoo H̲AAT ut met EW?*	Hoe gaat het met U?

English	Pronunciation	Dutch Spelling
How do you say___?	*hoo ZEKT ew___?*	Hoe zegt U___?
How far is___?	*hoo VEHR iss___?*	Hoe ver is___?
how much	*hoo-VAYL*	hoeveel
How much does this cost?	*HOO-vayl KAWST dit?*	Hoeveel kost dit?
hundred	*HAWN-durt*	honderd
hungry		
I am hungry	*IK hep HAWNG-ur*	Ik heb honger

I

I	*IK*	ik
I am___	*ik BEN___*	Ik ben___
I have___	*ik HEP___*	Ik heb___
I would like to___	*ik WIL HRAAK___*	Ik wil graag___
May I have___?	*MAHK ik___ HEB-un?*	Mag ik___hebben?
ink	*INKT*	inkt
in Dutch	*in ut HAW-lahnts*	in het Hollands

English	Pronunciation	Dutch Spelling
iodine	*YO-dee-um*	jodium
is	*ISS*	is
He is___	*hai ISS___*	Hij is___
Is it___?	*ISS ut___?*	Is het___?
It is___	*TISS___*	Het is___
It is not___	*tiss NEET___*	Het is niet___
What's that?	*waht IZ daht?*	Wat is dat?
What's this?	*waht IZ dit?*	Wat is dit?
it	*ut*	het

K

kilometer	*kee-lo-MAY-tur*	kilometer
knife	*MESS*	mes
know		
I don't know	*ik WAYT ut neet*	Ik weet het niet

L

large	*HROHT*	groot
laundry	*wahss-uh-RAI*	wasserij
laxative	*lahk-SAYR-mid-ul*	laxeermiddel

58

English	Pronunciation	Dutch Spelling
leave		
When does the train leave?	*hoo LAAT vur-TREKT duh TRAIN?*	Hoe laat vertrekt de trein?
left	*LINKS*	links
to the left	*naar LINKS*	Naar links
like		
I would like to___	*ik WIL HRAAK___*	Ik wil graag___
lost	*vur-DWAALT*	verdwaald
I am lost	*ik ben vur-DWAALT*	Ik ben verdwaald
luck		
Good luck!	*ut BEST-uh!*	Het beste!

M

Madam	*muv-ROW*	mevrouw
main street	*HOHFT-straat*	hoofdstraat
many	*VAYL*	veel
map	*KAART*	kaart
Will you draw a map?	*WILT ew un KAART TAYK-nun?*	Wilt U een kaart tekenen?

English	Pronunciation	Dutch Spelling
market place	*MARKT-plain*	marktplein
matches	*LEW-see-vayrss*	lucifers
mattress	*ma-TRAHSS*	matras
may		
May I have___?	*MAHK ik___ HEB-un?*	Mag ik___hebben?
May we have___?	*MO-hun wuh___ HEB-un?*	Mogen wij___ hebben?
Maybe	*miss-HEEN*	Misschien
meat	*VLAYSS*	vlees
mechanic	*may-ka-neesh-YEN*	mecanicien
milk	*MEL-uk*	melk
minute		
Wait a minute!	*WAHKT ay-vun!*	Wacht even!
Miss	*yuf-ROW*	Juffrouw
Miss Smit	*YUF-row SMIT*	Juffrouw Smit
Monday	*MAAN-dahk*	Maandag
morning	*MAWR-hun*	morgen
Good morning	*hoo-dun MAWR-hun*	Goeden morgen

English	Pronunciation	Dutch Spelling
mosquito net	*KLAHM-boo*	klamboe
movie	*bee-o-SKOHP*	bioscoop
When does the movie start?	*hoo LAAT buh-HINT duh bee-o-SKOHP?*	Hoe laat begint de bioscoop?
Mr.	*muh-NAYR*	Mijnheer
Mrs.	*muv-ROW*	Mevrouw
much	*VAYL*	veel

N

name	*NAAM*	naam
My name is___	*main NAAM iss___*	Mijn naam is___
What is your name?	*hoo HAYT ew?*	Hoe heet U?
near	*DIKT-bai*	dichtbij
Is it near?	*ISS ut DIKT-bai?*	Is het dichtbij?
the nearest town	*ut DIKST-bai-zain-duh DAWRP*	het dichstbijzijnde dorp
needle	*NAALT*	naald
nine	*NAY-hun*	negen
nineteen	*NAY-hun-teen*	negentien

English	Pronunciation	Dutch Spelling
ninety	*NAY-hun-tuk*	negentig
no	*NAY*	neen
north	*NOHR-dun*	noorden
Which way is north?	*WAAR ISS ut NOHR-dun?*	Waar is het noorden?
not	*NEET*	niet
I don't understand	*ik vur-STAA ut NEET*	Ik versta het niet
It is not___	*tiss NEET___*	Het is niet___

O

o'clock		
one o'clock	*AYN EWR*	een uur
of		
five of six	*VAIF vohr ZESS*	vijf voor zes
quarter of five	*KWART vohr VAIF*	kwart voor vijf
one	*AYN*	een
onions	*OU-yun*	uien

P

paper	*pa-PEER*	papier

English	Pronunciation	Dutch Spelling
past		
half past four	*HAHL-uf VAIF*	half vijf
quarter past three	*KWART o-vur DREE*	kwart over drie
ten past two	*TEEN o-vur TWAY*	tien over twee
pay		
I shall pay you	*ik ZAHL ew buh-TAA-lun*	Ik zal U betalen
pears	*PAY-run*	peren
peas	*EHR-tun*	erwten
pen	*PEN*	pen
pencil	*PAWT-loht*	potlood
pepper	*PAY-pur*	peper
pillow	*KUSS-un*	kussen
pins	*SPEL-dun*	spelden
safety pins	*VAY-luk-haits-spel-dun*	veiligheidsspelden
pharmacy	*ah-po-TAYK*	apotheek
pipe	*PAIP*	pijp
plate	*BAWRT*	bord
Please	*ahss-tew-BLEEFT*	Alstublieft

English	Pronunciation	Dutch Spelling
Point out the way to me	*WILT ew muh duh WEK WAI-zun?*	Wilt U mij den weg wijzen?
policeman	*po-LEET-see-ah-hent*	politieagent
police station	*po-LEET-see-bew-ro*	politiebureau
polish		
shoe polish	*SKOON-smayr*	schoensmeer
pork	*VAR-kunz-vlayss*	varkensvlees
porter	*KROU-yur*	kruier
post office	*PAWST-kahn-tohr*	postkantoor
potatoes	*AAR-dahp-ul-un*	aardappelen
pump (for water)	*PAWMP*	pomp

Q

quarter	*KWART*	kwart
quarter past three	*KWART o-vur DREE*	kwart over drie
quarter of five	*KWART vohr VAIF*	kwart voor vijf
Quickly!	*VLUK!*	Vlug!
Come quickly!	*KAWMT ew VLUK!*	Komt U vlug!
Go quickly!	*HAAT ew VLUK!*	Gaat U vlug!

64

English	Pronunciation	Dutch Spelling
	R	
railroad	*SPOHR-wek*	spoorweg
railroad station	*staash-YAWN*	station
raincoat	*RAY-hun-yahss*	regenjas
razor	*SKAYR-mess*	scheermes
razor blades	*SKAYR-mesh-yuss*	scheermesjes
repeat		
Will you repeat?	*WILT ew ut hur-HAA-lun?*	Wilt U het herhalen?
rest		
I would like to rest	*ik WIL HRAAK RUST-un*	Ik wil graag rusten
restaurant	*RESS-to-rahnt*	restaurant
Where is a restaurant?	*WAAR ISS un RESS-to-rahnt?*	Waar is een restaurant?
right	*REKTS*	rechts
To the right	*naar REKTS*	Naar rechts
river	*ree-VEER*	rivier
road	*WEK*	weg

English	Pronunciation	Dutch Spelling
Which is the road to___?	*WEL-kuh WEK haat naar___?*	Welke weg gaat naar___?
room	*KAA-mur*	kamer

S

safety pins	*VAY-luk-haits-spel-dun*	veiligheidsspelden
salt	*ZOWT*	zout
Saturday	*ZAA-tur-dahk*	Zaterdag
seat		
Have a seat!	*HAA ZIT-un!*	Ga zitten!
seven	*ZAY-vun*	zeven
seventeen	*ZAY-vun-teen*	zeventien
seventy	*ZAY-vun-tuk*	zeventig
shave		
I would like to be shaved	*ik WIL muh HRAAK laa-tun SKAY-run*	Ik wil mij graag laten scheren
shaving brush	*SKAYR-kwahst*	scheerkwast
shaving soap	*SKAYR-zayp*	scheerzeep

66

English	Pronunciation	Dutch Spelling
she	*ZAI*	zij
sheets	*LAA-kunss*	lakens
shirt	*HEMT*	hemd
shoes	*SKOO-nun*	schoenen
shoe laces	*SKOON-vay-turss*	schoenveters
shoe polish	*SKOON-smayr*	schoensmeer
shoemaker	*SKOON-maa-kur*	schoenmaker
sick	*ZEEK*	ziek
Sir	*muh-NAYR*	Mijnheer
six	*ZESS*	zes
sixteen	*ZESS-teen*	zestien
sixty	*ZESS-tuk*	zestig
sleep		
I would like to sleep	*ik WIL HRAAK SLAA-pun*	Ik wil graag slapen
slowly	*LAHNK-zaam*	langzaam
Speak slowly	*SPRAYKT ew LAHNK-zaam*	Spreekt U langzaam
small	*KLAIN*	klein
So long	*DAHK*	Dag

English	Pronunciation	Dutch Spelling
soap	*ZAYP*	zeep
shaving soap	*SKAYR-zayp*	scheerzeep
soup	*SOOP*	soep
speak		
Speak slowly	*SPRAYKT ew LAHNK-zaam*	Spreekt U langzaam
spoon	*LAY-pul*	lepel
start		
When does the movie start?	*hoo LAAT buh-HINT duh bee-o-SKOHP?*	Hoe laat begint de bioscoop?
station	*staash-YAWN*	station
Where is the station?	*WAAR ISS ut staash-YAWN?*	Waar is het station?
police station	*po-LEET-see-bew-ro*	politiebureau

Maastricht, Mheer

English	Pronunciation	Dutch Spelling
Stop!	*STAWP!*	Stop!
Straight ahead	*REKT-out*	Rechtuit
strawberries	*AART-bay-un*	aardbeien
street	*STRAAT*	straat
main street	*HOHFT-straat*	hoofdstraat
street car	*TREM*	tram
sugar	*SOU-kur*	suiker
Sunday	*ZAWN-dahk*	Zondag

T

tailor	*KLAYR-maa-kur*	kleermaker
take		
Take me there	*WILT ew muh DAAR naar TOO BRENG-un?*	Wilt U mij daar naar toe brengen?
Will you take me to a doctor?	*WILT ew muh naar un DAWK-tur BRENG-un?*	Wilt U mij naar een dokter brengen?
Will you take me to the hospital?	*WILT ew muh naar ut ZEE-kun-houss BRENG-un?*	Wilt U mij naar het ziekenhuis brengen?

Former Stads- or Latijne School, Nijemegen

Oldest house, Oisterwijk (Tilburg)

English	Pronunciation	Dutch Spelling
take a bath		
I would like to take a bath	*ik WIL muh HRAAK BAA-dun*	Ik wil mij graag baden
tea	*TAY*	thee
telegraph office	*tul-uh-HRAAF-kahn-tohr*	telegraafkantoor
telephone	*tul-uh-FOHN*	telefoon
ten	*TEEN*	tien
Thank you	*DAHNK ew*	Dank U
that	*DAHT*	dat
That is___	*DAHT iss___*	Dat is___
What's that?	*waht IZ daht?*	Wat is dat?
there	*DAAR*	daar
Take me there	*WILT ew muh DAAR naar TOO BRENG-un?*	Wilt U mij daar naar toe brengen?
they	*ZAI*	zij
They are___	*zuh ZAIN___*	Zij zijn___
think		
I think so	*ik huh-LOHF vahn WEL*	Ik geloof van wel

English	Pronunciation	Dutch Spelling
I don't think so	*ik ḥuh-LOHF vahn NEET*	Ik geloof van niet
thirsty		
I am thirsty	*IK hep DAWRST*	Ik heb dorst
thirteen	*DEHR-teen*	dertien
thirty	*DEHR-tuḳ*	dertig
this	*DIT*	dit
This is not___	*DIT iss NEET___*	Dit is niet___
This is too___	*DIT iss tuh___*	Dit is te___
This is very___	*DIT iss HAYL___*	Dit is heel___
What's this?	*waht IZ dit?*	Wat is dit?
thousand	*DOU-zunt*	duizend
thread	*DRAAT*	draad
three	*DREE*	drie
Thursday	*DAWN-dur-dahḳ*	Donderdag
time		
What time is it?	*hoo LAAT iz ut?*	Hoe laat is het?
tired	*MOO*	moe

English	Pronunciation	Dutch Spelling
I am tired	*IK ben MOO*	Ik ben moe
to		
to a doctor	*naar un DAWK-tur*	naar een dokter
to the hospital	*naar ut ZEE-kun-houss*	naar het ziekenhuis
To the left	*naar LINKS*	Naar links
To the right	*naar REKTS*	Naar rechts
tobacco	*TA-bahk*	tabak
today	*vahn-DAAK*	vandaag
toilet	*WAY SAY*	W.C.
Where is the toilet?	*WAAR ISS duh WAY SAY?*	Waar is de W.C.?
tomorrow	*MAWR-hun*	morgen
too expensive	*tuh DEWR*	te duur
tooth paste	*TAHNT-pa-staa*	tandpasta
toothbrush	*TAHN-dun-bawr-stul*	tandenborstel
towel	*HAHN-dook*	handdoek
town		
the nearest town	*ut DIKST-bai-zain-duh DAWRP*	het dichstbijzijnde dorp
train	*TRAIN*	trein

English	Pronunciation	Dutch Spelling
When does the train leave?	*hoo LAAT vur-TREKT duh TRAIN?*	Hoe laat vertrekt de trein?
Tuesday	*DINZ-dahk*	Dinsdag
twelve	*TWAA-luf*	twaalf
twenty	*TWIN-tuk*	twintig
twenty-one	*AYN-en-twin-tuk*	een-en-twintig
twenty-two	*TWAY-en-twin-tuk*	twee-en-twintig
two	*TWAY*	twee

U

understand		
Do you understand?	*vur-STAAT ew ut?*	Verstaat U het?
I understand	*ik vur-STAA ut*	Ik versta het
I don't understand	*ik vur-STAA ut NEET*	Ik versta het niet
underwear	*AWN-dur-hoot*	ondergoed

V

veal	*KAHL-ufs-vlayss*	kalfsvlees
vegetables	*HROON-tun*	groenten

73

English	Pronunciation	Dutch Spelling
very	*HAYL*	heel
village	*DAWRP*	dorp

W

wait

Wait a minute!	*WAHKT ay-vun!*	Wacht even!
warm	*WAHRM*	warm

wash up

I would like to wash up	*ik WIL muh HRAAK WAHSS-un*	Ik wil mij graag wassen
Watch out!	*LET awp!*	Let op!
water	*WAA-tur*	water
boiled water	*huh-KOHKT WAA-tur*	gekookt water
drinking water	*DRINK-waa-tur*	drinkwater
hot water	*WAHRM WAA-tur*	warm water
we	*WAI*	wij
We are___	*wuh ZAIN___*	Wij zijn___
We have___	*wuh HEB-un___*	Wij hebben___

English	Pronunciation	Dutch Spelling
May we have____?	*MO-ḫun wuh____ HEB-un?*	Mogen wij____ hebben?
Wednesday	*WOONZ-dahḳ*	Woensdag
welcome		
You're welcome	*tawt ew DEENST*	Tot Uw dienst
well (for water)	*PUT*	put
what	*WAHT*	wat
What's that?	*waht IZ daht?*	Wat is dat?
What's this?	*waht IZ dit?*	Wat is dit?
What time is it?	*hoo LAAT iz ut?*	Hoe laat is het?
when	*hoo LAAT*	hoe laat
When does the movie start?	*hoo LAAT buh-ḨINT duh bee-o-SKOHP?*	Hoe laat begint de bioscoop?
When does the train leave?	*hoo LAAT vur-TREKT duh TRAIN?*	Hoe laat vertrekt de trein?
where	*WAAR*	waar
Where are____?	*WAAR ZAIN____?*	Waar zijn____?

English	Pronunciation	Dutch Spelling
Where is___?	*WAAR ISS___?*	Waar is___?
Where is there___?	*WAAR ISS ur___?*	Waar is er___?
which		
Which is the road to___?	*WEL-kuh WEK ḫaat naar___?*	Welke weg gaat naar___?
Which way is north?	*WAAR ISS ut NOHR-dun?*	Waar is het noorden?
workman	*AR-bai-dur*	arbeider
would like		
I would like to___	*ik WIL ḤRAAK___*	Ik wil graag___
wounded	*ḫuh-WAWNT*	gewond

Y

yes	*YAA*	ja
yesterday	*ḤISS-tur-un*	gisteren
you	*EW*	U
Are you___?	*BENT ew___?*	Bent U___?
Have you___?	*HAYFT ew___?*	Heeft U___?